Big Bang SCIENCE EXPERIMENTS

BRIGHT IDEAS

THE SCIENCE OF LIGHT

Jay Hawkins

WINDMILL BOOKS

New York

Published in 2013 by Windmill Books, An Imprint of Rosen Publishing
29 East 21st Street, New York, NY 10010

First Edition

Editors: Joe Harris and Samantha Noonan
Illustrations: Andrew Painter
Step-by-Step Photography: Sally Henry and Trevor Cook
Science Consultant: Sean Connolly
Layout Design: Orwell Design

Picture Credits:
Cover: Shutterstock: left (clearviewstock) and right (Pete Pahham). Corbis: center (Mike
Kemp/Rubberball/Corbis).
Interiors: NASA: 4–5. Gianni A. Sarcone and Marie-Jo Waeber: 28, 29. Pinsharp 3D
Graphics: 30, 31 (Pixelshack), 32.

Library of Congress Cataloging-in-Publication Data

Hawkins, Jay.
 Bright ideas : the science of light / by Jay Hawkins. — 1st ed.
     p. cm. — (Big bang science experiments)
 Includes index.
 ISBN 978-1-4777-0320-5 (library binding) — ISBN 978-1-4777-0362-5 (pbk.) — ISBN
978-1-61533-670-8 (6-pack)
 1. Optics—Experiments—Juvenile literature. 2. Light—Experiments—Juvenile
literature. I. Title.
 QC360.H39 2013
 535.078—dc23
                                                   2012026224

Printed in China

CPSIA Compliance Information: Batch #AW3102WM: For Further Information contact Windmill Books, New York, New York at 1-866-478-0556
SL002558US

CONTENTS

SHINE ON! 4

WOBBLY LENSES 6

KALEIDOSCOPE 8

HALL OF MIRRORS 11

A BOX FULL OF SKY 14

3-D GLASSES 16

MAKE A PINHOLE CAMERA 18

LIGHT TOP 20

MAKE YOUR OWN ZOETROPE 23

RAINBOW MAKER 26

TRICK YOUR EYES! 28

GLOSSARY 30

FURTHER READING AND WEBSITES .. 31

INDEX 32

This book should shine a light on things!

SHINE ON!

THE BIG SQUEEZE

This cloud of dust and gas is found in the constellation of Monoceros. In some places, the cloud will become more and more closely packed. Eventually, it will become so dense that it turns into an incredibly hot substance called plasma. A star is born!

This picture shows a "stellar nursery" far across our galaxy. Parts of this cloud will one day transform into stars like our Sun! This book is packed with facts and experiments exploring the science of light.

TRAVELING LIGHT

Light travels faster than anything else in the Universe. It can speed along at nearly 186,000 miles (300 million meters) in a second. However, the cloud in this image is so far away that even at that speed, the light has taken 13,000 years to reach Earth!

TIME AND SPACE

Did you know that when you look at the night sky, you are traveling through time? The light from the stars takes years or even thousands of years to reach the Earth. So, when you look up at the stars you are literally looking into the distant past.

WOBBLY LENSES

Did you know that it's possible to bend light? Find out how for yourself by making some weird, wobbly lenses from gelatin!

YOU WILL NEED:

* 1 packet of gelatin (cubes or powder)
* Plastic containers with different shapes
* Hot water
* A flashlight
* A large piece of clear plastic (we used a shelf from the refrigerator)
* A cardboard box taller than the length of your flashlight
* A piece of thin, white cardboard measuring 16 x 12 inches (400 x 300 mm)

Step 1

Follow the instructions on the gelatin packet, but use half the regular amount of water.

Step 2

Pour the gelatin into plastic containers. Try some containers with flat bottoms, and others with curved bottoms.

Step 3

Tilt a flat-bottomed container to make a wedge-shaped lens.

Ask an adult to help with the hot water!

Step 4

Wait for the gelatin to set. When it is ready, briefly dip the molds in warm water to loosen up the gelatin.

Step 5

Turn the containers out onto a sheet of clear plastic.

Step 6

Switch on the flashlight and place it in a cardboard box, pointing upward.

Step 7

Position some white cardboard so that the flashlight beam shines across it.

We've fixed our cardboard to a chair.

Step 8

Place the transparent plastic on the box. Position different gelatin shapes above the flashlight to see how they bend the light.

HOW DOES IT WORK?

Light passes through different substances at different speeds. In this case, the light from the flashlight travels at different speeds through the air and through the gelatin. When the speed of light changes, it bends at the point where the two different substances meet. This is called refraction. You can change the direction of the refracted light with different shaped lenses.

7

KALEIDOSCOPE

YOU WILL NEED:

★ A paper towel tube

★ Compass

★ Paper and thin black cardboard

★ A pen or pencil

★ Mirrored cardboard

★ A ruler

★ Scissors

★ Tape

★ Colored tape

★ A thumbtack

★ Plastic wrap

★ Tracing paper

★ Small pieces of colored cellophane

★ Colored wrapping paper

Make thousands of crazy, colorful patterns with your own kaleidoscope!

Step 1

Draw around the bottom of a paper towel tube onto a piece of paper. Open your compass so the point is on the circle and the pencil is exactly in the middle. Draw the shape shown with dotted lines. Mark in the base of the triangle, then measure this line. The other two lines of your triangle should be this exact length.

Step 2

Using a ruler, draw a rectangle the same length as the cardboard tube onto the back of the mirrored cardboard. Mark off three parts with the same width as the sides of the triangle you drew.

Step 3

Fold the mirrored cardboard along the lines, to form a triangular shape. The mirrored side should be on the inside. Slide it into the paper towel tube.

Step 4

Draw around the end of the tube onto a piece of black cardboard. Cut out the circle, using scissors.

Step 5

Make a hole in the center of the circle. Stick it on the end of the tube with tape.

Make the hole with a thumbtack.

Step 6

Turn over the tube. Stretch plastic wrap over this end, and fix it in place with tape.

Step 7

Cut a 1 inch- (25 mm-) wide strip of thin cardboard and tape it around the end of the tube. Make sure it stands out a little from the end of the tube.

Step 8

Place some small pieces of colored cellophane on top of the cling film.

We finished it off with red tape.

Soon you'll be watching crazy patterns!

9

Step 9

Draw around the bottom of the tube onto tracing paper. Cut out the circle, leaving a gap of about half an inch (12 mm). Cut small flaps around the edge. Place this shape over the top of the tube and stick down the flaps with tape.

Step 10

Decorate the tube with colored paper.

Step 11

Hold your kaleidoscope up to the light. Look through the hole and turn the tube. What do you see?

HOW DOES IT WORK?

Light normally travels in a straight line. When it hits a mirror, it bounces off it in a different direction—this is called reflection. In a kaleidoscope, the light bounces around back and forth off the walls, creating many, many reflections of the colorful objects inside.

HALL OF MIRRORS

Have you ever been to the carnival and looked in the crazy mirrors? They can make you look tall, short, wide, slim, or just plain weird! Now, you can make your own crazy mirrors at home.

YOU WILL NEED:

★ A big, shiny spoon

★ 2 shallow cardboard boxes (e.g. shoe box lids)

★ Four sheets of thin, mirrored cardboard

★ Tape

★ Scissors

★ A craft knife

★ Mounting putty

★ Thin, black cardboard

Step 1

Look at your reflection in a shiny spoon. What differences can you see between the reflections on each side?

This kind of curved surface is called CONCAVE.

This kind of curved surface is called CONVEX.

Step 2

Let's make some mirrors to see those effects more clearly! Line the sides of a shallow cardboard box with black paper. Strengthen the corners with tape.

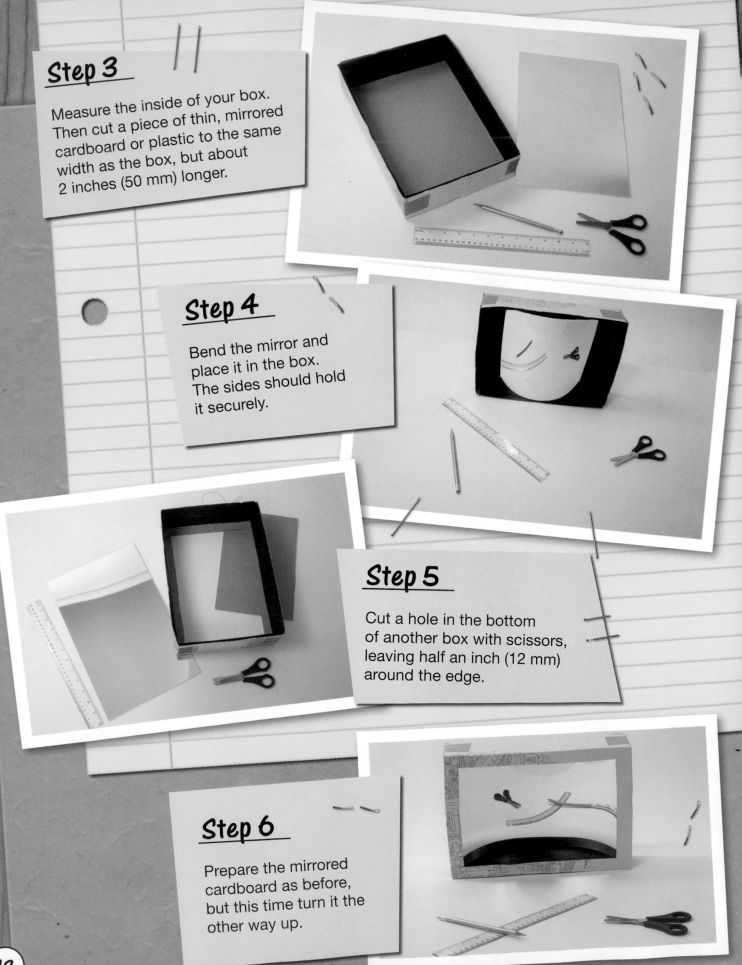

Step 3

Measure the inside of your box. Then cut a piece of thin, mirrored cardboard or plastic to the same width as the box, but about 2 inches (50 mm) longer.

Step 4

Bend the mirror and place it in the box. The sides should hold it securely.

Step 5

Cut a hole in the bottom of another box with scissors, leaving half an inch (12 mm) around the edge.

Step 6

Prepare the mirrored cardboard as before, but this time turn it the other way up.

Step 7

Ask an adult to help you score some mirrored cardboard in different ways, using a craft knife.

Step 8

Stick the pieces of mirrored cardboard onto a black or colored piece of cardboard, using mounting putty. Decorate the frames with colored paper. Now you have four mirrors ready for your hall of mirrors!

HOW DOES IT WORK?

When light hits the surface of a mirror, the direction of the reflected light depends on the shape of the mirror. If a mirror bulges outward, it is called convex. Convex mirrors make objects look stretched. If a mirror bends inward, it is called concave. Concave mirrors make objects look smaller, or even flip them upside down! It depends on how far away you stand.

Does this reflect well on me?

A BOX FULL OF SKY

Have you ever wondered why the sky is blue when it is lit by the Sun, which looks orange? Here is a simple experiment that explains it all.

YOU WILL NEED:

★ A large, clean, glass or plastic container
★ A flashlight
★ A spoon
★ Milk
★ Water
★ Books

Step 1

Fill the container three quarters full of water. Add a little milk to the water, and stir it with a spoon.

Step 2

Position the flashlight on some books, so that it shines through the the middle part of the water.

Step 3

Shine the flashlight through the water, but stand to the side of the beam. Keep adding milk to the water and stirring. After a while, the light will turn blue.

The milky water in our experiment acts like the sky.

Step 4

Now stand in front of the flashlight. The beam will look orange!

HOW DOES IT WORK?

When the sun shines through the atmosphere, light of different colors is bounced around by air particles. Blue-colored light gets bounced around more than light of any other color, so whichever direction you are looking from, the sky appears blue. The same thing happens in our experiment, when light is bounced around by the milk.

Red and yellow light is bounced around much less than blue, so when you look at the beam of the torch, it looks orange. The sun looks orange for the same reason.

3-D GLASSES

View amazing 3-D pictures through your own handmade glasses!

YOU WILL NEED:

★ Thin cardboard

★ Red and blue-green colored plastic sheets from a craft store

★ Tape

★ A glue stick

★ Scissors

★ The 3-D images on pages 30–32

Step 1

Copy the template opposite, and cut out the three parts of the glasses. Score along the dotted lines.

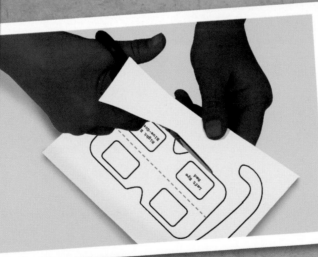

Step 3

Fold the earpiece flaps along the dotted lines and fix to the frame with a glue stick or tape.

Step 2

Cut out two rectangles of colored plastic— one should be blue-green and the other red. Tape them to the glasses.

Step 4

Fold the frame down to seal in the lenses and the earpiece flaps. Secure them with tape.

HOW DOES IT WORK?

The blue-green lens makes it hard to see blue and green, but you can still see red. The red lens does the opposite. Your brain tries to make sense of the different images each eye is seeing by turning them into a 3-D picture!

TURN TO PAGES 30-32 TO FIND SOME 3D IMAGES!

LEFT EYE RED

RIGHT EYE BLUE-GREEN

Make sure red is on the left, blue-green on the right.

MAKE A PINHOLE CAMERA

This crazy camera will flip your world upside down! It is based on the very first cameras.

YOU WILL NEED

★ A box with a lid, such as a shoebox

★ Black paper

★ Tape

★ Scissors

★ A thumbtack

★ A sheet of wax paper

★ A small cup

Step 1

Make sure that no light can get into your box once the lid is on. Tape up any holes or joins.

Don't put the lid on yet!

Step 2

Draw around a small cup or mug at one end of the box and cut the circle out with scissors.

Step 3

Cut a rectangle out of the other end of the box.

The rectangle is 1 inch (25 mm) smaller each way than the end of the box.

Leonardo da Vinci used a camera similar to this!

Step 4

Cut out a square of black paper or kitchen foil a little bigger than the circular hole. Then tape it to the inside of the box to cover the hole.

Step 5

Use a thumbtack to make a small hole at the center of the black paper.

Step 6

Cut out a piece of wax paper a little bigger than the rectangular hole and tape the wax paper to the inside of the box. This is your screen.

Step 7

Fix the lid on with tape.

HOW DOES IT WORK?

When light passes through a small hole, the picture on the other side always ends up upside down because of the way the light rays pass through it. This is the same thing that happens in the pupil of the eye, but our clever brains flip the image around in our heads for us!

Step 8

Your pinhole camera is ready to use! Point it at something bright and look through the hole at the screen.

The picture is upside down!

LIGHT TOP

Make a terrific top that changes color before your eyes as it spins around!

YOU WILL NEED:

★ Old CDs or DVDs
★ Marbles
★ Tape
★ A hard surface
★ A pencil
★ Scissors
★ Pens or paints
★ Colored paper

Did someone say "marbles?" I lost mine years ago!

Step 1

Draw round a CD or DVD on colored paper. Cut out several circles. Also cut out the holes in the middle.

Step 2

Stick a paper disk to the CD or DVD with a gluestick.

Step 3

Fix a marble in the central hole of the disk with small strips of tape. Test spinning it on a hard surface, such as a kitchen worktop.

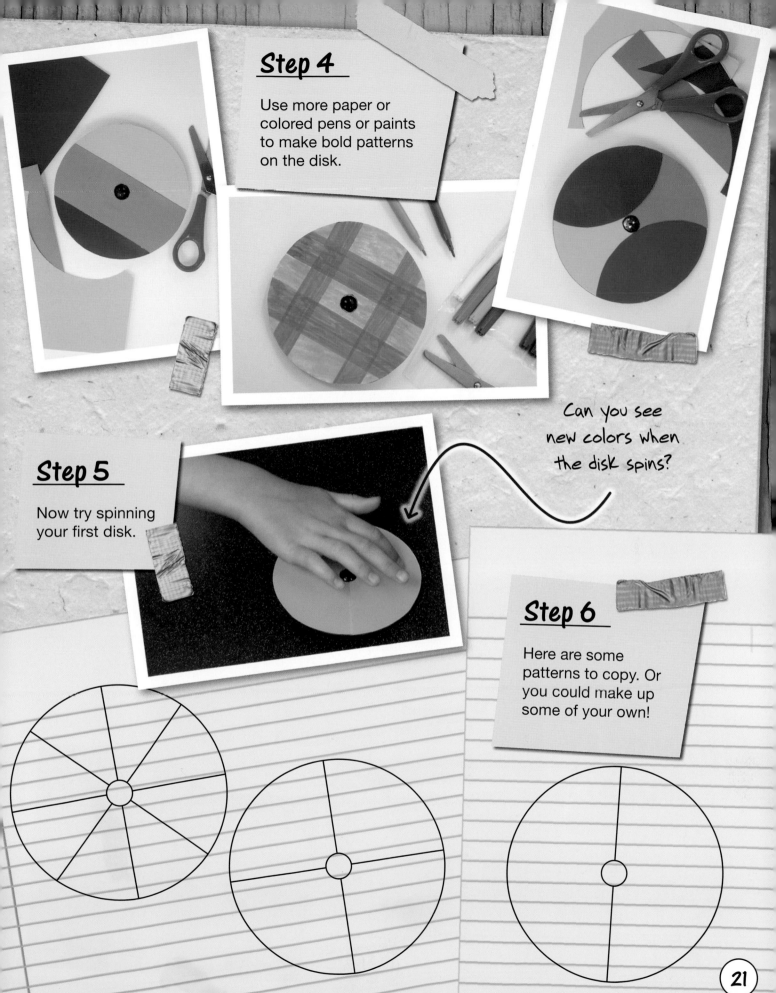

Step 4

Use more paper or colored pens or paints to make bold patterns on the disk.

Can you see new colors when the disk spins?

Step 5

Now try spinning your first disk.

Step 6

Here are some patterns to copy. Or you could make up some of your own!

21

Here's a way to make neat segments.

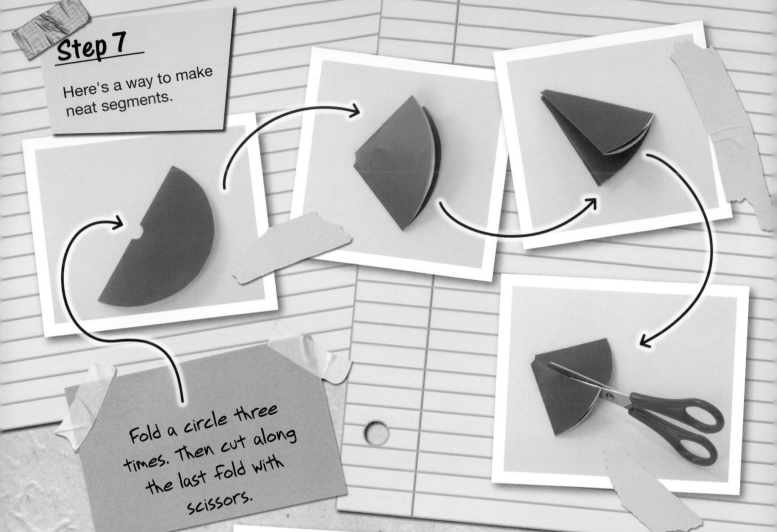

Fold a circle three times. Then cut along the last fold with scissors.

HOW DOES IT WORK?

What happens if you make a spiral pattern?

When the top whirls around really fast, you can see all the colors, but your brain can't separate them. So what you see is a blend of all the colors mixed together.

MAKE YOUR OWN ZOETROPE

Have you ever dreamed of being an animator? You can make a start here by creating your first ever moving picture!

YOU WILL NEED

- ★ A circular box (such as a cheese box) with a lid
- ★ Modeling clay
- ★ A map pin
- ★ A small button
- ★ A piece of cork
- ★ Tape
- ★ A ruler
- ★ A pencil and pen
- ★ Black paper and white paper
- ★ Colored paper or tape

Step 1

Poke a hole in the center of a circular box and its lid with a map pin.

Use a ruler to find the exact center.

Zoe Trope? I think I went to school with her.

Step 2

Put some modeling clay around the edge of the inside of the box, to add weight.

Step 3

Push the map pin through the lid, through the hole in a button, through the bottom of the base, and into a cork beneath. The box should now spin freely on the lid.

Step 4

Cut a piece of black paper about 2.5 inches (65 mm) high which will fit around the inside edge of the lid.

Trim the paper to exactly fit the lid.

Step 5

Draw lines along the black paper about 1 inch (30 mm) apart. Following those guidelines, cut slots about 1.5 inches (40 mm) deep.

Step 6

Stick the black paper in place with tape. Then cut a piece of white paper, about 1 inch (25 mm) wide, to fit inside it. Don't stick it down yet!

Step 7

Draw guidelines along the white paper about 1 inch (25 mm) apart. Draw a series of pictures in the "frames" you have marked out.

A repeated action that joins up at the beginning and end will work well.

Step 8

Spin the zoetrope and watch your animation through the slits.

You could decorate the outside of the box with colored paper or tape.

HOW DOES IT WORK?

When you spin the zoetrope, you can see each of the pictures one at a time in very quick succession. Your brain tries to make sense of what your eyes take in. It interprets these rapidly changing pictures as movement, so you see a continuous moving picture.

RAINBOW MAKER

You don't need to wait for rain to see a rainbow anymore. Here is how to make a nice, dry one indoors. You may not find a pot of gold at the end, though!

YOU WILL NEED:

★ Some old CDs

★ A sunny day, or if this is not possible, a flashlight

★ A window with curtains or blinds

★ White paper

Step 1

Find a sunny window. Close the blind or curtain, but leave a little gap to let a direct sunlight in.

My pet chameleon just loves rainbows.

Step 2

Hold a CD, shiny side up, in the beam of sunlight.

Step 3

Reflect the light onto a piece of white paper.

Step 4

Change the angle of the CD. You will see a variety of different rainbow patterns.

Step 5

You can use a flashlight if it's not a sunny day, but the rainbows might not be as bright.

HOW DOES IT WORK?

When white light passes through a triangular prism, it splits into all the different colors of the rainbow. The surface of a CD is made of plastic with lots of tiny ridges above a mirrored surface. These act like lots of tiny prisms arranged in a circle, so when light hits the surface of the CD, it makes a rainbow.

TRICK YOUR EYES!

Sometimes what you see is not all it seems. You can play tricks on your brain and eyes with these fun optical illusions!

Step 1

Look closely at this picture. Does it look like the spirals are moving around?

Step 2

Try turning the page around in a circle. What can you see now? It should look like the circles are vibrating and turning slightly.

Step 3

Look at the rabbit in the middle of this picture. Does it look as if the spots are rippling and moving?

HOW DOES IT WORK?

A phenomenon such as an optical illusion tricks us because the different cells and receptors in the eyes receive and process information at different rates. As a result, the brain can sometimes receive a false image based on the information arriving at varying speeds.

Malfunction! My visual systems are not working properly.

GLOSSARY

atmosphere (AT-muh-sfeer) The layer of gases surrounding a planet.

concave (kon-KAYV) Describing a curved surface that bulges inward.

convex (kon-VEHKS) Describing a curved surface that bulges outward.

lens (LENZ) A curved piece of glass or other transparent material that changes the direction of light passing through it.

phenomenon (fih-NAH-muh-non) An observable fact or event.

plasma (PLAZ-muh) A state of matter that is different from the usual solid, liquid, or gas.

prism (PRIH-zum) A piece of glass or other transparent material with smooth, angled sides that change the direction of light passing through.

receptor (rih-SEP-ter) A cell in the eye that receives light and sends information on to the brain.

refraction (rih-FRAK-shun) The process by which light changes direction after passing through an object.

stellar (STEH-ler) Having to do with stars.

Look at these pictures through your 3-D glasses (pages 16-17)!

FURTHER READING

Brasch, Nicolas. *Tricks of Sound and Light.* Science Behind. Mankato, MN: Smart Apple Media, 2011.

Claybourne, Anna. *Light and Dark (Why It Works).* Philadelphia, PA: W. B. Saunders, 2012.

Kessler, Colleen. *A Project Guide to Light and Optics.* Newark, DE: Mitchell Lane, 2011.

Nunn, Daniel. *Shadows and Reflections.* Chicago, IL: Heinemann, 2012.

Sandall, Barbara R. and Logan, LaVerne. *Light and Sound: Energy, Waves, and Motion.* Greensboro, NC: Mark Twain Media/ Carson-Dellosa, 2010.

Silverman, Buffy. *Let's Investigate Light.* Vero Beach, FL: Rourke Publishing Group,2012.

Whiting Jim. *Light (Mysteries of the Universe).* Falls Church, VA: Creative Education, 2012.

Websites

For web resources related to the subject of this book, go to: www.windmillbooks.com/weblinks and select this book's title.

INDEX

3-D 16, 17

Air 4, 5, 10, 19, 20, 21, 25

Animation 23, 25

Atmosphere 15

Brain 17, 19, 22, 25, 28, 29

CD 20, 26, 27

Colors 8, 9, 10, 14, 15, 20, 21, 22, 23, 27

Concave 11, 13

Convex 11, 13

Flashlight 6, 7, 14, 15, 26, 27

Galaxy 4

Kaleidoscope 8, 10

Lens 6, 7, 16, 17

Light rays 19,

Mirror 8, 10, 11, 12, 13, 27

Moving pictures 23, 25

Optical illusion 29

Pinhole camera 18, 19

Plasma 4

Prism 27

Pupil 19

Rainbow 26, 27

Receptor 29

Reflection 11, 13, 27

Refraction 7

Stellar "nursery" 4

Zoetrope 23, 25

Look at this picture through your 3-D glasses!